Ardor

OTHER BOOKS BY

MARVIN BELL

———————

The Book of the Dead Man (Vol. 1) [1994]
A Marvin Bell Reader: Selected Poetry and Prose [1994]
Iris of Creation [1990]
New and Selected Poems [1987]
*Drawn by Stones, by Earth, by Things that Have Been
in the Fire* [1984]
Old Snow Just Melting: Essays and Interviews [1983]
*Segues: A Correspondence in Poetry
(with William Stafford)* [1983]
These Green-Going-to-Yellow [1981]
Stars Which See, Stars Which Do Not See [1977]
Residue of Song [1974]
The Escape into You [1971]
A Probable Volume of Dreams [1969]
Things We Dreamt We Died For [1966]

Ardor

THE BOOK OF THE DEAD MAN

VOLUME 2

MARVIN BELL

COPPER CANYON PRESS

The publication of this book was supported by
grants from the Lannan Foundation, the National Endowment for the Arts,
and the Washington State Arts Commission, and by contributions from
Elliott Bay Book Company, James Laughlin, and the members of
the Friends of Copper Canyon Press.
Copper Canyon Press is in residence with Centrum
at Fort Worden State Park.

Library of Congress Cataloging-in-Publication Data

Bell, Marvin 1937–
Ardor: the book of the dead man, volume 2 / by Marvin Bell
p.cm.
ISBN 1-55659-081-4 (pbk.)
1. Title.
PS3552.E52B65 1997
811′.54–DC20 93–43415

COPPER CANYON PRESS
POST OFFICE BOX 271 · PORT TOWNSEND · WASHINGTON 98368

Grateful acknowledgment is made to the editors of books and periodicals in which the following pieces, some in earlier versions, appeared previously:

Agni Review: #66

Bloomsbury Review: #54

The Colorado Review: #42, #57 and #60

Contemporary American Poetry, 6th edition, Houghton-Mifflin: #53 (section 1)

Dog Music: A Poetry Anthology, St. Martin's Press: #46

Electronic Poetry Review: #38 and #64

Five Points: #70

The Gettysburg Review: #44 and #63

The Gift of Tongues:

Twenty-Five Years of Poetry from Copper Canyon Press: #43

Good Company: American Poets Born Between 1935 *and* 1945, Maypop Press: #58

Gray Spider Press (broadside): #43

The Great Blue Heron and Other Poems, Adrienne Lee Press: #45

Great River Review: #39 and #65

Harvard Review: #62

Hayden's Ferry Review: #38 and #64

The Iowa Review: #51 and #53

Left Bank: #67

Minutes of the Lead Pencil Club, Pushcart Press: #37 (section 2)

New American Zeen: #47

The New Republic: #58 (section 1)

The North Stone Review: #37, #43 and #55

Orbis (England): #54

Outsiders, Milkweed Editions: #58

A Poem of One's Own, Middlebury College Press/
University Press of New England: #70

Poetry: #68

Poetry East: #34

Poetry Miscellany: #45

Prairie Schooner: #36 and #47

spelunker flophouse: #48

Telling and Remembering: A Century of American Jewish Poetry,
Beacon Press: #58

Trafika (Prague): #34, #40, #43, #48 and #61

Verse: #49 and #56

Voices on the Landscape, Loess Hills Press: #34

The Writing Path, University of Iowa Press: #34, #40 and #61

DOROTHY, NATHAN, JASON, LESLIE, COLMAN

CONTENTS

Live as if you were already dead.

Zen admonition

———————

For a long time pure linear painting drove me mad
until I met Van Gogh, who painted neither lines nor shapes
but inert things in nature
as if they were having convulsions.

ARTAUD: *"Van Gogh: The Man Suicided by Society"*

———————

To be at all – what is better than that?

WALT WHITMAN

PREFACE

——————————

Before the Dead Man, minus-1 was still an imaginary number.

The Dead Man is that much more alive for being alive and dead at the same time. Thus, the distance has narrowed between the known and the unmentionable. That is, blood runs thicker than water, and the Dead Man is like bread for gravy.

The Dead Man knows who made love under the rising cloud of Vesuvius. The Dead Man was there when the Trojans fell for Helen. He knows that a stain in the earth may carry the genetic code for a lifetime of maladies, and he flings himself again and again on the ground to leave something to others. Things go, time goes, while the Dead Man stays.

The Dead Man is not a persona, not a mask. The Dead Man will not be organized by a box or a circle, a sign or a sum. His quantum, millennial presence-absence permits him to travel in the dark matter of space and in the sticky stuff of an atom.

Microscopics and macroscopics. Oddly transported.

It will be the absolute precision of the thing that undoes the thing. Likewise, our minds traveling any distance to the unseen rub up a fog and a static. Hence, with no-mind, with no strings attached, perfected in fallibility, brimful and teeming, the Dead Man ardently inhales the beginning and the end.

The Dead Man's perspective rattles the cage of literature and yearns to be useful without, a tool by which to meditate beyond conjecture. *The Book of the Dead Man* is but a basic work, fundamental. Let those who can make use of it excerpt and reshape it. Let those who can stand it, stand on it. As commentary, it welcomes more commentary. The Dead Man stands on the target, watching the world betray itself for a quiver of arrows. He, not I, has doused the light that made the dark impenetrable.

M. B.

Ardor

THE BOOK OF THE DEAD MAN (#34)

1. About the Dead Man, Ashes and Dust

The dead man is slag ash soot cinders grime powder embers flakes
chips slivers snippets lava and sand.
He is fumes fog smoke and vapor.
Do not mistake the exhausted dead man for the mangled, dissolved
or atomized.
His mark is not a blemish on the earth but a rising tide of
consciousness.
His tracks are not the footprints in the foyer but thoughts brought
to bear.
The letter of the dead man impedes, but the letter and the spirit of
the dead man together animate.
The dead man is not the end but the beginning.
To conceive of the dead man is the first act of birth, incipient.
The dead man was first.
At the table, nothing more can be poured into his empty bowl.
His is the whisper that cannot be traced, the hollow that cannot be
leveled, the absolute, the groundless ideal, the pure – in all
respects, the substance of the honorific.
That is, everything outside the dead man is now inside the dead man.

2. More About the Dead Man, Ashes and Dust

The dead man, Ladies and Gentlemen, clears his throat.
He adopts the rhetorical posture of one to whom things happen.
He rises, he appears, he seems to be, he is.
It is the dead man's turn to toast the living, his role to oversee the
merriment, his part to invoke the spirits and calculate the
dusk.

He is recondite in the dun evenings, deep in the sallow dawn, fit for
      contemplation all day, he is able to sit still, he lets his dreams
      simmer in the milky overcast of a day commonly pictured.
Who but the dead man has better drawn the covers over his head?
What better could the dead man have done to show his good will
      than to keep his secrets buried?
No one hath done as much.
Consider where the dead man goes at the end of the day.
Picture his brusque exits, reconsider his gruff respects, listen to his
      last words that found the nearest ear.
When the dead man clears his throat, it may be first words or last
      words.
When there is no birthday, no anniversary, no jubilee, no spree, no
      holiday, no one mass, meeting or service, then naturally it is
      up to each person whether to go ahead or turn back.
The dead man is 360 degrees of reasoning, three sides of a
      syllogism and four sides of a simple box.

THE BOOK OF THE DEAD MAN (#35)

1. About the Dead Man and Childhood

In an evening of icicles, tree branches crackling as they break
      frozen sap, a gull's bark shattering on snow, the furnace
      turned down for the night, the corpse air without exits –
      here the dead man reenters his fever.
The paste held, that was dry and brittle.
The rotting rubber band stuck to the pack of playing cards to keep
      it together.
In the boy's room, the balsa balanced where there had once
      been glue.
Recognition kept its forms in and out of season.
Why not, then, this sweaty night of pursuit?
He has all of himself at his disposal.
He has every musical note, every word, though certain notes of the
      piano have evaporated.
Shall he hear them anyway?
The dead man's boyhood home withholds from its current
      occupants the meaning of desecration, nor shall they be the
      destroyers of the past in their own minds.
You too have seen anew the giant rooms of the little house in which
      you were a child.
You have seen the so-heavy door that now barely resists a light
      hand.
You have walked down the once endless corridors that now end
      abruptly.
Were you so small then that now you are in the way?
You too sat at the impossibly high kitchen table with your feet
      dangling, drawn down by the heavy shoes.
All this and more the dead man remembers the connective
      quality of.
In those days, there was neither here nor now, only there and the
      time it would take to reach it.

2. More About the Dead Man and Childhood

After Adam ate the apple, there was one more, and then one
    more....
After Orpheus looked back, there was another and another....
The dead man discerns betwixt and between, he knows mania and
    depression, he has within him the two that make one, the
    opposites that attract, the summer pain and the winter pain.
He walks both the road of excess and the least path, and lives most
    in the slow-to-ripen spring and extended autumn.
The dead man does not come when called but tries to hit a baseball
    in the dusk.
He does not yet know he wants to ride the horse that took the bit in
    its mouth.
He lives in the attic and the big closet where the radio parts and the
    extra glassware hold their codes.
He is the initiate.
He feigns nothing, he has nothing else in mind, later he will be
    charged with having been a boy.
Even now, in May and September he feels the throbbing tissue of
    that fallow world from which he was forced to be free.
The dead man in adulthood knows the other side, and he winces at
    the fragility of the old songbooks, taped and yellowed, held
    there in time.

THE BOOK OF THE DEAD MAN (#36)

1. Drinking Glass, Pencil and Comb

This dead man's threesome is the true menagerie.
The dead man's menagerie represents the dead man's provisions,
    the expression and appearance of them.
When the dead man runs his finger up and down the teeth of a
    comb, it makes a zippy glissando.
An undercurrent of gnawing attends his ruminations because he
    chews his pencil.
The glass holds scissors, pens and pencils, a feather and other
    breakaway items.
If Socrates had never used a cup except to hold a few trinkets, the
    dead man would not now ponder the natural utility of
    objects.
If Diogenes had not carried a lantern, the dead man would not seek
    the genuine, the authentic and the valid in the bafflement of
    himself.
Oh, if there had been no pencil in the first place, no vessel, no tool
    of any sort, the dead man would not have had to travel by an
    oblique path to the end.
To gather, to say, to be shaped – in a glass, with a pencil, by a comb.
To speak or draw, to cough or *harumph* – the dead man designates
    forms of expression with and without words.
What has the dead man gathered in cups and vases, in bowls and
    glasses?
Do the missing teeth of his comb alter the musical scale?
Will the pencil have been fingerprinted, the graphite carbon-dated?

2. More About the Dead Man's Drinking Glass, Pencil and Comb

The dead man's comb shall fall from favor, his glass shall kiss
another's lips, his pencils shall find other words to whisper.
The dead man holds up one hand to ward off the accidental
collections, the detritus, the used-up but not discarded, but
of course the world piles on.
The dead man as event, person or place is the leftover, the extra, the
abundance too great for salvage, the too-much here and the
little-enough there.
The dead man, like the Hundred Years War, persists in the years
following.
The dead man remains, like Diogenes' lantern, in the dark.
The dead man perseveres the way the Roman Empire keeps falling,
with the music, the culture, the barbaric visitations, the
evidence, the premonitions.
The dead man knows that each hemisphere of the brain acts in the
light of conviction.
He has seen the contests of history: the insurgent peace, the one-
sided negotiation, the unrecovered casualties, the tongue left
in the goblet.
The dead man's relics are primitive by any standard.

THE BOOK OF THE DEAD MAN (#37)

1. About the Dead Man and Little Much

High density sunshine adds weight to the dead man's eyelids.
Some say it's the humidity, but it's the heat.
The dead man, watching the surface percolate, charts the seepage.
It's the heat, it's the torpor of the day, it's the high cost of living.
The dead man is waysoever into lifting and living, what with
      pressure bearing down and the rushing about overhead to
      forget.
The dead man considers the greater good of the ne'er-do-well, the
      greater story never told, the seven sins, the seven wonders,
      the seven dwarfs, ancient expectations, previous versions, the
      discontinued, the remaindered, the deleted, the disappeared.
He, the dead man, being in fever and ardor, confirms that the
      frivolous is mixed up with the earnest, the make-believe with
      actuality, the old with the new, the living with the dead.
The dead man has littlemuch language for these precocious times.
What an era: the dead man poling for the bottom finds it
      fathomless.
For it was the nature of ethics to need language, however
      littlemuch.
The dead man has all the languages, the scripts, those based on
      sound, those based on picture, those based on interval, those
      soaked in adrenaline, those dry as English toast.
The dead man knows how hard it can be to speak with a mouthful
      of grit.
The dead man doesn't spit straight up.

2. More About the Dead Man and Little Much

It's little enough to be voiceless in a clamor.

The dead man shapes the din and the uproar, he puts potholes
along the information superhighway, he blocks the ramps, he
disconnects, he is off-line, he interferes.

The dead man knows the roads and the music, the wires and the
keys, are there only to make the rats run faster.

The dead man tries on one hat at a time, he is persistence of vision
incarnate, he is knowing of the binary two-step, he is
formidably with-it, he is hip but he knows better.

The promises of knowledge, this genetic free-for-all, these complete
records, this Big Brother that has your number, this non-
stop news, this access, this roundly thumped privacy – the
dead man witnesses each incursion into the far reaches of
ignorance.

He thinks at this rate the gauges will break and the computers
crash.

He sees the sundials wobbling nervously over what time it is.

He sees the stars leaning.

To the dead man, nothing more is something else, a concept beyond
population and resources, an idea whose time is past.

He has littlemuch lingo, littlemuch answers, littlemuch solar
longevity.

Whereby the dead man rocks the planet to sleep, the song still on
his lips, his covenant unbroken.

THE BOOK OF THE DEAD MAN (#38)

1. About the Dead Man and Sap

The dead man will not add 1 + 1.

He squeezes things that settle near him until they drip a little.

The dead man's things shine with an oil pressed from the raw flakes
      of beached fish, the ripe carcasses of birds that winter would
      not release, the everyday jam and jelly of who wants what.

Who and the dead man have felt the earth heave though the air was
      still?

Who and the dead man have made their bed and lie in it?

It is a panoply, a plethora, a surplus, a surfeit, an abundance, a
      bounty and an earthly prosperity.

The dead man cut his hand caressing the scaled hearts of catfish
      and trout, he stiffened from gripping the back of the crab
      while its claws clicked, his joints display the geology of labor
      and love-making, he is wrinkled from laughter and stained
      from tears.

When there is no more wrinkling and weeping, no physiognomy of
      pleasure, no anticipation, no abundance, nothing extra, then
      okay it's the way it is, not the way we remember.

2. More About the Dead Man and Sap

The milk, juice and pitch of the dead man ebb and flow.

Lifting and falling, the dead man's inner ocean cleanses him of
      wanderlust, his days abroad now a ghostly apparition.

The dead man is fascinated by mirages, oases, missing tide pools,
      lost lakes, basins where rivers ran, wells that went dry.

He sees his face in the mud of a drained marsh.

The dead man does not plant his flag in the dust but doubles back
      like reflected light.

Pity naïve Narcissus, bent to a river that was moving on.

If there is a bit of froth, foam or lather, a few suds, an escaped
    bubble, a globule of blood anywhere, the dead man will find
    it and begin again.
The dead man finds it fortunate to have been in the train station
    when the coffin was loaded and the mourners toasted the
    departed who was just leaving.

THE BOOK OF THE DEAD MAN (#39)

1. About the Dead Man and the Interior

When the dead man's arm goes numb, he thinks an emotion is
  leaving.
Feeling the loss of feeling, he thinks he feels less than he did
  before.
The dead man lived on whatever made him say *mmm* but now he'll
  exist less overtly.
Ashes are the dead man's contrition, dust is his handkerchief.
No, it's otherwise: contrite dust, handkerchief in ashes.
Some issues for the dead man: whether he is fish or reptile,
  whether he is milk or glue, how inadvertent his chemistry.
The dead man pulls the blanket up around his shoulders, then
  stretches a leg out to offer the cold a corridor inward.
He waits to see things the other way around: handkerchief turning
  to dust, contrition gone up in ashes, et cetera.
He observes the anniversary of the ushers when they come to
  replay their roles in the carriage of time.
Then the dead man was soft, but a year afterward he has been eaten
  away like an irradiated worry-stone.
The dead man's flesh, that blanketed all feelings, gives no further
  indication of his countless emotions.
All about the dead man, nickels collide with quarters and pennies
  with dimes.
For all who attended the dead man, none carries a key to the
  interior.

2. More About the Dead Man and the Interior

The dead man is the forked bearer of a swaddling cloth, many
    blankets, the needlework of immunity and an ironed
    winding-sheet.
His Jew's-harp jawbone held the music in place.
His Semitic sternum contained that final heartbeat for which all
    preceding heartbeats were a ceremonial preface.
When there is no more accidental, no inadvertence, no
    anthropological terrain sufficiently confined, no chaos
    unlinked to further chaos, no anarchy within anarchy, no
    thing of discrete substance, then nothing may come between
    thought and feeling.
Why did the dead man believe he was losing feeling when all he was
    losing was an uncontrollable shiver?
How was he supposed to know that the car was a coffin?
Why did the dead man step on the gas when the tank was empty?

THE BOOK OF THE DEAD MAN (#40)

1. Socks, Soap and Handkerchief

The dead man is haunted by socks and soap.
Socks and handkerchiefs pile up in his cabinet and fill his thoughts.
The dead man wears away like socks in shoes or soap in water.
Dead man's soap has a wind chill factor of room temperature.
Dead man's socks have holes in them where the toes went.
The dead man's handkerchief is a textbook in geometry.
What, to the dead man, means what, what with time passing
     muster?
The dead man twisted his wrist while trying to soap his back.
He sprained his ankles pulling up his socks.
He blew his brains out while using his handkerchief.
The dead man is feet-first, he is clean as wax, he is comforted.
The dead man wears socks on his hands to effect the look of
     mittens.

2. More About the Dead Man's Socks, Soap and Handkerchief

The dead man slid on soap, eased his way, stepped with care, wiped
     his glasses until they were too clear to see.
The dead man depends on his socks to match.
He loves to strip the wrapper from a bar of soap.
He puts himself through the wash-and-rinse cycles of the seasons.
He wipes and wipes the blades of his knife and repacks them.
The dead man feels loss, aging and grief – socks, soap and
     handkerchief.
He fulfills the expectations of maids, seamstresses and laundresses.
He sees the soaps replaced, the socks darned, the handkerchiefs
     refolded.
To the dead man, socks without holes are a sign of worldly cares.

To the dead man, soap follows the loss of innocence.
The dead man carries a handkerchief for show, for no reason, to
        have it to drop, to have it to pick up.
The dead man, gathering the used and lost, adds one more.

THE BOOK OF THE DEAD MAN (#41)

1. About the Dead Man and Hot Topics

Reactive, resurgent, the dead man welcomes a steamy updraft.

Must all he's been amount to something?

What, going uphill, is the dead man's loftiest position?

Give him his organic druthers, his fleshy fast action, his dual feelings.

Let him lie down in your top spot, for he shall make its
    whereabouts known.

What was in the offing when, hearing his heart tick, the dead man
    wondered, Where truth and beauty?

Feeling his rib cage quiver, the dead man wondered, What thread,
    what stroke?

For he hath warred with the pebbles and the roots.

By turns, the dead man sprang upon himself, buoyed himself,
    suffered himself, sank within himself and rose from himself.

The dead man is intimate with grubs.

He sniffs the soggy earth, ingesting vapors of blood and semen.

The dead man bursts like spring in retaliation.

He endorses the behavior of the lower animals.

He cheers those who bed down on the pulpy forest floor and those
    who pursue their dreams.

Who more than the dead man savors the soft interior of an enigma?

The dead man, forced to live on abstract rations, chose love.

Was it God, or was it the wine?

The dead man, thumping within as if he might jump out of his skin,
    waits out the beats, outlasts the interval, all the time acting
    as if he were the lowest common denominator, the very one.

When there is no more regularity, no bottle of seeds, no injection of
    pollen, no gauze to map the outpouring, no tourniquet to
    staunch the expression, no crutch, no illness or health, then
    okay why not truth and beauty, why not blameless, helpless
    truth and beauty?

Tell me that, says the dead man, tell me, why not that?

2. More About the Dead Man and Hot Topics

The dead man has a bone to pick.

Gripping a wishbone, arming a slingshot, facing a fork in the road, the dead man takes no sides, off in all directions, divergent from yes and no, should and shouldn't, will and won't.

In his immersible dungeon, divining the shafts of waterways, calculating time and tangent, the dead man relentless deploys his effects.

A piece of the dead man is down the road a piece.

Naturally, he will not vanish, naturally.

Nor will the dead man be delivered, he is habitually the remains.

The dead man's day heats up with the first glimpse of the familiar.

All is familiar to the dead man in the shimmering waterways of the sun's fire.

All is wholly met by the dead man in the shining inferno of the tides.

Shall now his entire being stare into the fire, shall now he sit like a sea shell, shall now he tremble like a petal?

To the contrary, the dead man rises to shave the light layer by layer.

Few shall be given to fathom the dead man's passion.

The dead man frees his subjects – topical treatments fair in method and random in result.

The dead man does not wince at the touch of time, nor does he finagle to bring to light the compensations, tips and rewards, nor the grainy gratifications that dissolve in unfixed emulsions.

When there is no more this and that, no indoors or out, no originals, no effigies, no copycat lump of stone set to bang out the new universe, nothing top or fancy, why then the dead man has all there is of hot topics.

The dead man loves you because your brain kills him.

THE BOOK OF THE DEAD MAN (#42)

1. About the Dead Man's Not Telling

The dead man encounters horrific conditions infused with beauty.
He looks and sees, dare you see with his unblinkered eyes.
He sniffs and ingests, dare you do the same as he.
He hears and feels, dare you secure such stimuli and endure the
      heart.
He sets foot on the anomalies, he traverses the interior laden with
      the screams of witnesses underfoot.
He walks among the pines crackling with the soon-to-be-broken
      backs of new life.
He freely rests among the appetites of the unsatisfied.
He bites off the head of the Buddha.
The dead man has seen bad Buddhahood.
He has doubled back, he has come around, he has cut across, he has
      taken the long shortcut.
What is out there, that germinates?
The dead man knows that there is no luck but dumb luck, no heart
      that will not skip, no pulse that does not race.
Things go, time goes, while the dead man stays.

2. More About the Dead Man's Not Telling

Has not the dead man asked a basic question?
Did he not lie in the crib like a question mark without a sentence?
Did he not encode the vitality of roots, the beauty of leaves, the
      kinetics of branches, the rapture of the sun, the solace of the
      moon, even the hollow that shapes the seed?
The dead man is the one to ask when there is asking.
Those who invest in the past or future shall forfeit the dead man's
      objectivity, his elasticity strung from down-and-dirty
      to up-and-ready.

When the oracle spoke, the dead man listened like a shell.

When the quixotic signaled from the wood, the dead man grasped the new life that needed no more plasma than the dew.

How comely the horrific consequences, how amiable the gorgeous advantage of the newly born.

Things go, time goes, but the dead man goes nowhere without you.

You who told him know what is on the dead man's mind.

You at the fringe, the margin, the edge, the border, the outpost, the periphery, the hinterland, you at the extremity, you at the last, counterpoised, have caught the inference.

The dead man counts by ones and is shy before your mildest adoration.

THE BOOK OF THE DEAD MAN (#43)

1. About the Dead Man and Desire

When the dead man itches, he thinks he has picked up a splinter.
Unable to free himself of an itch, the dead man thinks he has a
　　splinter.
The dead man looks at a praying mantis and sees a pair of tweezers.
He offers himself to be walked on by claws.
He waits for the odd fox to trot across his chest and strings of ants
　　to scrape him pore to pore.
He anticipates the flaying action of chemicals and the sponge baths
　　of the rain.
The dead man, scoured, is the ruby servant of the vineyard.
The dead man is the salt of the earth, the dust and the sawdust, the
　　honey in the wine.
Hence, his thoughts must rise to the moon and beyond to take his
　　mind from that splinter if it is a splinter, that itch if an itch is
　　what it is.
Everything the dead man thinks has its other side.
The dead man thinks Saturn has been much married but forever
　　lonely.

2. More About the Dead Man and Desire

If he were just valves and glue, just honey and chocolate, just hot
　　and cold, the dead man's thoughts would not hop, skip and
　　jump so.
If he were just comparative, if he were absolute, if he knew his own
　　mind, the dead man's heart would not race so.
Who but the dead man wonders which of its moons Jupiter favors?
Who knows better than the dead man in his bones the pitch at
　　which the earth breathes?
The dead man is rapt before the altar of consciousness.
He enters the forbidden realms of experience without penalty.

To the dead man, there is something grave about umbrellas,
   something sinister about servitude, something debilitating
   about knowledge — like sunlight on slugs.
The dead man rolls back into place the rock that was moved to find
   out.
Like Sisyphus, the dead man wants what he has.
When there is no more meek, no vainglorious, no catch-as-catch-
   can, no inheritance, no opportunity knocking that is not also
   the wind, then naturally the dead man lives for love.
The dead man, fervent to feel, makes no distinction between a
   splinter and a stinger that cost something its life.

THE BOOK OF THE DEAD MAN (#44)

1. About the Dead Man and Humor

The dead man is very very laughing.

Why so whale of a jolly?

There's bustling and piercing that enticingly through the fabric of
daily lives went.

There's old-style regimes that Communist went the way of, and
Fascist repercussions the knowing of deserted and despaired.

Who from ancient times mystery has pondered, Latinate explosions
in the postscript.

He doesn't care who knows, what with letters to be forged.

The dead man turned and rolled, the red thread he conjured.

The dead man came upon a tree and of a while carving it, was
gentle but definite.

The letters he engraved there being grown now heatingly in the
sun, exposure unruly.

What is fair?

All there he said was x loves y and why not?

The dead man very very laughing to be open and thought.

2. More About the Dead Man and Humor

Too hard to be the only survivor terrifies.

Too much to become hands-up not making a move just to get by.

Winds, stars, flags, masks – all defy, furthering.

The dead man can't say this or that, this being roundly rubber-
banded to snap back, that too.

Into position the dead man takes up.

Wasn't lightning made the dead man glow, no flare-up suddenly.

Was unfleeting affection won him and gave him silly to be ofttimes
when nothing accounted for it but she side-by-side.

The dead man apologizes for breaking training, wrenching syntax,
    turning topsy-turvy to be laughing down.
The dead man knows that beneath and below overhead come
    round.
The dead man, puffed and filled, scampers like a frantic wasp, his
    oath held back because the moment is coming.
He laughs to be knowing when knowing is laughing, with the punch
    line riding up just in time.

THE BOOK OF THE DEAD MAN (#45)

1. About the Dead Man and the Great Blue Heron

When the dead man stands on one leg, he thinks he's a heron.

Wobbly, one foot out, the dead man thinks he's a heron but not
a fish.

As a fish, the dead man knows he doesn't have a leg to stand on.

Still, fishpicker of cold waters, the dead man is off-and-on goofy,
awhile whimsical or fitful, increasingly counter to the
sparrow as which he first flew.

Naturalists of the dead man, who once recorded the sparrow's vigor
and the exotica of the nightingale, now search the
archaeopteryx's stone remains, seeking to foretell the
strenuous operations of crane and cormorant, pelican and
albatross.

The dead man, birder of pigeons and crows, mimic of warbler and
whistler, favors in geezerhood the awkwardly limber, the
footfall of the fragile shinbone, the critical exactitude of the
next step.

What has happened to the dead man that he should turn sharply
from the liquid beauty of dead nature?

Who now will mark the sea-change that swirls about him?

There's this about the dead man, that he can be more or less.

He is, more or less, the heron that met a loon.

Habitual, the proximate flocks took stock until nightfall.

2. More About the Dead Man and the Great Blue Heron

The dead man, rickety, compelled to wade the shallows with a
hoarse croak for an anthem, still feels uplifted, transcendent,
ecstatic, blessed, sanctified and generally okeydokey.

The dead man has been the bird of paradise, which is why.

Why is also because he has known the breeze that carries seed from
the cottonwood in the spring and maple leaves from their
sugary cupboards in the fall.

Therefore, from whatever he was, or thought he was, in whatever
form faltering, it was there in the offing that fervor and peril
would walk together, burrow, swim and fly.

When there is no one body, no two bodies, no bird that was not a
fish, no fish that will not hover, no snake that cannot learn to
walk, no man or woman who did not crawl, then the possible
and the probable conjoin to grant the blue heron a step.

The dead man's golden eye reconnoiters fear and far, as he folds in
his neck to try flight.

With his neck-stretch and wingspan, the dead man will reach the
boundary waters of sense and apparition, all beneath an
infinite sky.

Why is the dead man transfixed by birds come to earth and the
great blue heron stilled by a wee trembling in the current?

Is it the goose bumps, is it the chill?

Why is because he is dizzy, not daft.

THE BOOK OF THE DEAD MAN (#46)

1. About the Dead Man's Dog

The dead man, *that* man, consorted with canines in the turmoil of a
    derangement sensed by few others.
The mongrel was apt, the mutt, the half-breed is best, the hybrid,
    the mixture − being those of an underclass to which the
    dead man belongs.
The dead man's dog is immediate, primary, without tedious human
    calculation.
The dead man's dog follows his nose, his tongue lags but
    accompanies, his owner's voice mixes with the sighing of the
    browning leaves.
The dead man's dog is housebroken, barnbroken, fieldbroken,
    lawnbroken but is free to go.
The dead man's dog keeps a tight leash on his master, dragging him
    to every clandestine murmur, every rumor of affection.
The dead man's dog has the wherewithal to violate those senseless
    codes meant to make a man or woman stay.
To the contrary, the dead man's dog shakes hands, he fetches, he
    heels, also he behaves and misbehaves in human
    proportions.
The dead man's dog plays dead.

2. More About the Dead Man's Dog

When there is no more approbation, no license, no all-time
    immunity, no obedience or disregard, no loyalty that is not
    also the pick of the litter, no luck but dumb luck then okay
    it's not a show, and spunk is what it takes.
It takes the dead man an eternity to romp, meanwhile he learns a
    mutt's moxie.

27

Oh pretty dogs that reap the rage of benefactors in good times.
Oh dogs shorn of the outdoors, oh clipped, oh shaggy shaggy
    shaggy.
The dead man's dog does not sit up and beg.
The dead man's dog is the hybrid of now and later, bred to be good
    with children, eager, vigilant.
Hound and buddy, enthusiast of dishes and scraps, perch for fleas,
    station of sanity, trained to disobey in the nick of time – the
    dead man's dog runs beyond reason.
His is the virtue of the undersides of logs.
He readies his bones for the passage to the underworld.
He rolls before the fireplace, the whole house his sarcophagus, his
    face lit like that of an Egyptian jackal.
The dead man's dog's teeth are nine-tenths of the law.
His claws are the quills whose marks will be the stuff of history.
His tail is a brush for which the wide day is his canvas.
Eagerly, the dead man lies down with dogs, observer of puppy love
    and dog song.
The dead man's dog is a little bit of all right, a wagging yes, a cause
    of whistling and waving, cupped hands and come-when-
    called.
He bestirs the dead man's fortitude.

THE BOOK OF THE DEAD MAN (#47)

1. Toaster, Kettle and Breadboard

The dead man lives in the flesh, in memory, in absentia, in fact and
fiction, by chance and by nature.
What are we to make of his continuous use of everyday objects?
For the dead man's fingerprints are everywhere: his crumbs, his
residue, the marks his tools made.
The dead man corks and uncorks the passable wine.
He needles the bad meat to make it tender, he breads the wings of
the chicken, he takes from the incendiary oven his meal at
leisure.
The dead man has no stomach for ordinary indigestion.

2. More About the Dead Man's Toaster, Kettle and Breadboard

The dead man sees fireweed grow from scorched ground.
He sees the conspicuous consumption of Thoreau, the torch-
bearing saviors of Walden.
He reckons up the passionate aesthetics devoid of the smell of
ashes.
He notes the footprints on the rice paper of those who seek divine
abstinence.
He records and distributes the knowledge of fair game.
Did the dead man eat roasted bread or drink from boiling water or
take a piece of something, leaving the rest?
There is only the evidence of the dead man's estate.
There is only the proof of toaster, kettle and breadboard.
The dead man does not confuse plain water with weak tea or piety
with indifference.

When there is no more appetite, no inhalation, no absorption, no
	osmosis, no digestion, then okay let the reverie commence in
	the ether.
The dead man lives in the meantime, the in-between time, the time
	it takes to boil, broil, bake and fry, assimilating the cooked
	and the raw, the beefy and the lean.
The dead man is himself an ample morsel-to-be, a tidbit, a
	sweetmeat, slices and scraps and a mouthful of quills.

THE BOOK OF THE DEAD MAN (#48)

1. About the Dead Man and Diminishment

Haply, the dead man has been reduced to the basics.

The diminution of a lifetime gives the dead man a way out.

Through the rafters of the trees there comes now a gentle buzzing,
a shy laughter, a faint murmur expressing the apathy of time.

To the dead man, antiquity is a law unto itself.

It is scored in the creases of palms and inscribed but faintly on the
undersides of eyelids.

The dead man merely mimics the modern affectation in being
"positively Medieval" about the fifth to fifteenth centuries.

The dead man knows that the buzzing is that of houseflies, not
honeybees.

He understands the futility of the field mouse and the laughter of
the owl.

He gauges the flight of the swift and the piecework of the predator.

For the dead man is the wizard of divination by the footpath of the
crosses.

The dead man is tucked in to ride out the epoch.

He is the long and short of it, the more or less of it, the changes
that were thought to be doomsday.

Beneath his fingernails is the debris of torches that were said to
hold eternal flames.

The dead man had the last straw thrown down upon him
innumerable times until he took the lot of it back to wheat.

He is the decaying cellulose and the throngs of microorganisms that
desert it.

His is the saliva that ate away the rafters, the nails, the gadgets, the
dingbats and the blueprints.

For the dead man is alternative, the possible reassembled as a
hollow sphere in which the bounce, sound and feel of it
depend upon the emptiness within.

Small as he is, little as he was.

The dead man's reticence, reluctance and restraint are as lucrative
    to him as all the tea in China and have the same effect.
But the dead man is happy to be sleepy.

2. More About the Dead Man and Diminishment

After tea, the dead man traces his chronology as well as those early
    trade routes that were the outer, overt primitive versions of
    synthesis.
The dead man, after tea, relearns the inner topography of his
    eyelids.
Who is to say that sleep is not the hollow of his ruminations?
Who would deny the dead man his afternoon shut-eye?
The dead man dozes to relive his vigor and the fantastical torpor
    of rest.
He snoozes to recall the drowsy aftermath of pleasurable storms.
No one but the dead man knows how passionately he fought in the
    arenas of solace and consolation.
It means this to be the dead man, the tablets agree.
The dead man, knowing that things end, is elated to be eternal.
Hence, the dead man sponsors all quirks and whims because glory
    is fleeting.
Because glory is fleeting, he trespasses on authority with impunity.
The dead man dances on the graves of the dour and the overly
    manicured.
When there is no more large or little, no unmarked brow, no
    unmapped eyelid, no white page, nothing ill-fated or
    rebuked, then the dead man rivals the nine muses of
    antiquity in being the root cause.
Physically speaking, the dead man's fragments are neither litter nor
    shreds but hyperbolic segments of minute organic activities.

That is, the dead man is too pleased to have it known, too joyful to
    say why, too intense to sleep late.
What is that clamor, that din, that uproar, that racket, that
    "wisecrack giving itself away as outcry"?
Is the dead man flavored or preserved, is he seasoned or is he
    cured?
Supine, not dormant, the dead man is prone to florid events in the
    atmosphere.
In the valley of divine wizardry, by the footpath of the crosses, it is
    the dead man who reckons diminution in lieu of time.
Kook, weirdo, oddball, nut, the dead man's makeup is one-part
    matter to one-part essence.

THE BOOK OF THE DEAD MAN (#49)

1. About the Dead Man and the Elusive

The dead man has not and, having not, has.

Why anyone cannot see this is anyone's guess.

The organist who said "dead man, dead man, dead man" again and
again, trying to expel it.

The man who wrote on the leaf of a gingko, "Here is death," as if it
were necessary to die to be green again, and it is.

The man who evaded and consigned, the woman who delegated and
lied, the expert who left out something, the initiate who
didn't know, the preacher with the scarred knees.

The benighted, who want more stuff.

Who, not being able to tell, spat out the essence with the excess.

Ah, happenstance, that made of contingency a condition.

Ah, the twinkling of an instant, that made a likelihood of chance.

Big boys all, come blow your horns.

The cat's ascended who could tell us why opposites are one.

The homeless man who left behind a note: "Even if I had money, I
would not buy *Anubis*, it frightens me so."

Who, asleep on the street, wrote: "I have been visited in dreams by
a fox, and once by an animal like a large weasel."

2. More About the Dead Man and the Elusive

You will not rid yourself of the dead man at the margins.

You will not evade him or replace him at the edges.

Try to write it between the lines, his method is your madness.

Paint it outside the borders, his character is your fault.

Are you one of those students who does the assignment but misses
the lesson?

The dead man drifts by in the aura of lost opportunity, pointing to
a better misstep.

Yes, it is all true – what he said, what he meant, what he only
       suggested, what he didn't let on about.

While he was about, you might have asked, but you did not.

Your well-groomed erudition made the sucking sound of a bog as it
       confirmed you and likewise drew you in.

Did you think approval was a sudden intake of air?

The dead man hears the relief sought by gasping, panting, whispers
       and wheezes.

His time is the space between two hands about to clap.

THE BOOK OF THE DEAD MAN (#50)

1. About the Dead Man and One or More Conundrums

Within range of the sodden fanfare.

A little fevered, to know in one's bones.

Undone, which is to say one awaits word in the province of eros.

The dead man has completed his task, he has hewn one capacious
Gordian knot, he has shaved head-to-foot with Occam's
razor, he has freely determined his immunity and renewed
his license.

It is requisite to read between the lines, who are able.

It is best to deduce and intuit, who are skillful.

It is apt to stay the course if one would see the flayed reclothed.

2. More About the Dead Man and One or More Conundrums

Enthralled, the dead man lay waste to the picayune by gathering
them into one.

To the dead man, the whole is partial and the partial whole.

One had only to watch the snow- or rain-fall to see the truth
exposed.

And what would the truth look like exposed?

Would it have sinew, would it have veins and arteries, would it throb
with inner organs, would it cough and speckle and freckle
and fret?

Would its dark hair turn white?

Would it labor, would it die?

The dead man is troubled by his close relationship to experience.

The dead man sees a conflict between experience and truth, as
between the dark matter of space and the sticky stuff of the
atom.

Particle upon particle the dead man heaps to slay the beast by its
own weight.

36

THE BOOK OF THE DEAD MAN (#51)

1. About the Dead Man and Taxidermy

Out of a suitcase of discards there came dead lilacs and a dead Abe
      Lincoln, and the dead man was there to see it.
From a posh trunk there spilled dead lilies and a dead Kennedy,
      and the dead man was there to see it.
From the heavens there rained explosives, and from the hills came
      the thud of mortars, and the Family of Man lay in pieces, and
      the dead man was there to see it.
The dead man studies taxidermy to better preserve the bailiwick.
He rearranges museums according to the ideals of moderation and
      proportion.
The dead man props a wax Plato by a cave on the road to town.
He puts a plaster-of-Paris bust of Aristotle by the gate.
He posts the heads of lions and elk on the top edge of the city wall.
He sends for the pickled brain of Einstein, the shreds of the
      dropped brain of Whitman.
He asks for a kidney stone taken from Pablo Neruda.
He runs ads seeking dried gall bladders, lung tissue, voice boxes,
      eardrums and stringy veins.
He offers a reward for information leading to a heart.
He bribes the guard to better examine the Pharaoh.
He rehearses the torture of slaves, pow's and prisoners of
      conscience to see where the parts fell, that he might retrieve
      them.
The dead man will put the world back together, wait and see.

2. More About the Dead Man and Taxidermy

It is as if you were a roustabout in outer space, collecting the burnt-
out hardware.
It is as if you had been given the last stick and nail and sent to the
beaches to draw forth wrappers and tops.
It is as if you had been given a carton of cigarettes to strip, the
papers to be buried, the tobacco to be scattered.
It is as if you were just body heat, just temporal resolutions, just a
mold without walls.
It is as if you had asked for it, as if you had missed a chance to
decline.
It is as if you were for a moment the eyes of a packed moose head,
one wing tip of a stuffed eagle, the whole jaw of a bear rug.
It is as if you were some fractured persistence, some ancient belief
in thought.
It is as if you were suddenly laughable, mournful and senseless.
It is as if you were one of a kind by default, who killed the Buddha,
contrived a less-than-ideal Plato, and mixed up Aristotle the
sentry with your comings and goings.
It is as if you were gone today and here tomorrow.
It is as if you were the last one, out looking for a tar pit so that later
they will know.

THE BOOK OF THE DEAD MAN (#52)

1. About the Dead Man's Contrition

The dead man's acquired cackle is a kind of repentance.

His smile fills the gap between what was said and what he heard.

The shock wave of his metaphysics, pursuant to temporal civilities, carries within it his sorrowful greeting.

That ardor with goose bumps, that love you that lay fallow, that passion for honey had to be cut short to survive.

Without penance, without reparation, without auras or whiteouts, neither active nor passive, the dead man's entreaties lift love from its matrix so that the lover can reach all the way around it.

The distance has narrowed between the known and the unmentionable.

2. More About the Dead Man's Contrition

It is as if the dead man employed a skull hammer to drive home his point.

It is as if he used a bone saw to separate the known from the unknown and a two-fingered wrench to grip the truth he once held in his teeth.

The dead man has slipped out of the lecture on flowers to explore a field.

He wends his way among specimen after specimen.

His apology may take the form of a basket of examples.

His explanation may seem an Etruscan code.

His exegesis may be no more than a pebble pitched into boiling lava.

What on earth! and How can he! and What next!

Folly to explain, what nonsense, what balderdash, what baloney.

Here lies the poetry of the twentieth century, consigned to a chauffeur who knew only the road to the cemetery.

THE BOOK OF THE DEAD MAN (#53)

1. About the Dead Man and the Cardboard Box

Low sounds roll over the dead man in his cardboard box.

Infernal steam hisses at the dead man in his refrigerator carton.

The dead man had a cardboard fort, a cardboard playhouse, a
      cardboard cutout, a paper doll, a boxful of shredded
      cardboard, now he makes a nest of excelsior.

Is the dead man the natural antecedent to homelessness?

Who else knows the fact, suspects the truth, surmises the outcome?

Who else can make change?

The dead man seeks no other shelter than this, the elements.

The dead man accepts no other refuge than this, this asylum, this
      retreat, this cloister.

Shall the dead man be buried alive – possibly.

Shall the dead man be left for dead – inevitably.

The dead man's cardboard box is a plaything next to the crates and
      cartons of the homeless, the car hulks, the infested
      comforters, the littered steam tunnels, the bins, the boards
      and the bags.

The dead man finds no trophy to the sublime in these ramshackle
      coffins.

The dead man refuses to go to his grave while people live like this.

He evacuates the heated halls of Congress for seats to sleep in.

He clears out office buildings, libraries, banks and post offices, and
      decrees that decrepit vagrancy shall find its home in
      government.

The dead man stifles deconstruction of the homeless.

2. More About the Dead Man and the Cardboard Box

The dead man goes home, he goes back to where he came from, he goes to hell, he goes to some trouble, he goes to pieces.

The dead man sees the homeless go without.

He sees the paper cups of soup carried into the dark hovels of the down and out.

He sees the blankets and bedrolls in doorways and the newspaper insulation left to curl on the steam grates.

He senses the relief in all-night subways, 24-hour waiting rooms, public restrooms.

He feels the sun restoring life after a cold night on the sidewalk.

He knows what it means to take medicine from a bottle.

The dead man hears the siren when they come to take a body from the street.

He goes to see but is shouldered aside by those who will take its place.

The dead man memorizes homeless math: one fewer means ten more tomorrow.

He sweeps up the broken vessels and used needles, the emptied sandwich wrappers, the paper and cardboard, the human waste.

He cleans up after those who have gone to make a living at the dumpster.

The dead man knows about salvage, scrap iron, scrap flesh.

The dead man is a homebody condemned to sleep in packing, fated to live among the derelict in the lap of luxury.

Shut in, locked out, germane or alien, the dead man enumerates the nomadic tribes of the cities – by box, blanket and bedbag.

The dead man finds out after the fact whether or not he has made the rent.

THE BOOK OF THE DEAD MAN (#54)

1. About the Dead Man and the Corpse of Yugoslavia

When the dead man feels nausea, he thinks he is in the Balkans.

Feeling nausea, the dead man thinks he is scattered body parts.

Dismemberment makes the dead man queasy – historically.

Is not the dead man a witness to every dole, lot and quota?

Was not the dead man in place when the Serbs shelled Sarajevo?

The dead man heard the shouts of the victims being pasted into
     history over brief captions.

He pointed a finger at the butcher Milošević when the guns
     hammered the old city.

He shook his clenched fist at the genocide visited upon the
     Muslims, as it was and would be upon the churches,
     synagogues and mosques of the secessionary and
     independent.

He twisted and thrashed to transmit an underground murmur of
     conscience.

He gyrated, he spun, he literally threw himself into the air, he did
     everything possible to gain their attention but dance.

At a distance, the dead man's screams made a beautiful music.

Now the dead man, having lain down in flash fire and fire storm,
     bewitches his contemporaries.

The dead man proffers the scent of something left undone, but
     there are so few words for how a thing smells.

The dead man is the last one of many.

2. More About the Dead Man and the Corpse of Yugoslavia

The dead man sees the head, then the heart, of a dismembered
State.
He sees the arms that tried to clap, the eyes that blinked and went
blank and were turned under.
He raises a fluttering flag held by the leg bone of the violated.
He hangs the dry tongues of the multitudes along the fences of
western Europe.
He mails the ears and lips to the West for overnight delivery.
The dead man is the inscriber of names and dates, the conveyor of
last wishes and words, secretary to a truce signed over the
scent of cremation.
When there is no more defense, no strategic withdrawal, no
bargain, no outcome, no resolution, then of course there's no
condemnation, no horror, no moral reality, nothing
intangible to impute dishonor to the victors.
The dead man is the spoils to which the victors pledge their
allegiance.
The dead man wonders why the hurry?
Meanwhile, the dead man certifies each eye extracted for an eye,
each tooth for a tooth: the whole carnivorous escapade.
The dead man picks among the living for future specimens.

THE BOOK OF THE DEAD MAN (#55)

1. About the Dead Man and Famine

When the dead man feels pangs, he thinks he is in the Sudan or
      Somalia when the crops failed.
Feeling hunger pangs, the dead man thinks he is all bones.
Hollow cheeks give way to no-cheeks, a flat abdomen fills with air.
Witness the dead man fall in, line up, relinquish and shrink.
Was not the dead man taller once, heftier, closer to heaven?
The dead man passes his hands through the shadows of sagging
      flesh.
He points a skeletal forefinger at the water carrier and the cook.
He quivers from cold, trembles when the trucks thunder in with
      rations.
He pulls himself up by a gossamer thread connected to tomorrow.
He stands in the food line like a construct of bones half hidden by a
      dropcloth.
The dead man's stomach no longer rumbles.
Dried-up potions, bags of totemic remains, cosmetic invocations to
      universal powers, letters to the authorities now weight the air
      – immobile, debilitating artifacts.
The dead man sniffs the air with the last of his lung power.
His chips, shreds and tatters will be the good luck charms of
      leftover believers.
The dead man neither believes nor doubts but is nourished by half-
      measures.
The dead man is free to go.

2. More About the Dead Man and Famine

The dead man's condemnation would be for all time, so he does not condemn.

The look in the dead man's eyes widens to encompass four food groups, five grains, seeds and sauces, livestock and prey.

His famine is not a fast.

He rouses himself for a meal, he transforms his geometric figure – triangles, trapezoids – into the number "1," he jingles and jangles as if he were a dancer festooned with jewelry, but it is only the click clacking of loosened tongue and groove.

This is not purgation but the good intentions of the fearful.

Who but the dead man can convey salutes, cheers and accolades to the starving in Somalia, the Sudan, those living in the eroding landfill from which the good stuff has been taken?

Who better than the dead man to welcome the Malthusians?

When there is no horrifying number, no catastrophe that cannot be miniaturized, no news too big for a box, no lack more immediate than others, then the dead man does not linger.

The dead man wonders not why but who.

He files the forms that will be found afterward, he fills in the blanks that will furnish the data, he obliges by coming to a full stop.

The dead man wonders not what but when.

THE BOOK OF THE DEAD MAN (#56)

1. About the Dead Man and the Jury

Hast thou witnessed what the dead man hath witnessed, seeing the
    killer go blameless and free?
Is it only that the dead man sees him slither, slide and sneak, dodge
    and deceive, fake and feint, equivocate and prevaricate, and
    is that anything?
Is it simply, or satisfactory, that the dead man's weary of witnessing,
    and is that anything?
The dead man witnesses the coronation of the coroner – sovereign
    of fact's residue – sanding the rust from the knife, polishing
    the bones, distilling the flesh, boiling the bravado, taking the
    measure of man, but is that anything?
There sits the jury, replete, fraught, brimming, abundant, and the
    dead man wonders, What is conscience?
Before them appears the judge, obvious, absolute, his robes of
    conviction billowing as he walks in a murmuring breeze, and
    the dead man wonders at the wherewithal that endowed
    every creature but mankind with resolution.
The dead man banks the fees and delays, the sidebars, the recesses,
    the motions and objections, the appeals and sentences, the
    fines, the imprisonments, the executions, and with one strike
    of his gavel turns them all into dust.
Is it anything at all, the dead man asks, to bear the sword and
    scales, to wear the blindfold, to ask and answer, to overrule
    and sustain, to swear, to promise, to pledge, to bargain, to
    settle?
Is there any for or against?
The dead man takes neither hostage nor loot, yet he has emptied
    the vaults of their value, and he causeth the pricey counsel to
    cower with self-knowledge.

When there is nothing but the client's good suit, the jury's self-
　　doubt, the time since the crime, the charts and photos, the
　　measurements and samples, then what knowledge is on trial,
　　what rote redundancy passes for fact, what past lingers?
Where there is no more overriding impulse, no search for the truth
　　that is not a battle to the death, no word left to meaning, no
　　uncontested jurisdiction, no unacceptable flimflam, how then
　　is a spinoff, a byproduct, an effect less significant than its
　　cause?
The dead man did not yell "Fire!" in a crowded theater.
He did not utter the word "containment" during times of genocide.
He did not use the conditional tense to describe the human
　　condition, nor does he undermine the paralytic, the
　　catatonic, but awaits an underground reckoning.
The dead man and his fellow dead are the jury whose verdict will
　　out.
It is not the dead man's doing when a sentence contains the seeds
　　of revolution.
The dead man was the first to arm the sentence.

2. More About the Dead Man and the Jury

When nothing more can be done, when the jurors have sunk into
　　the sublime humus, the soft undergarment, the liquid center,
　　the tender moment, the pliant interpretation, then guilt is
　　merely innocence with an attitude.
The dead man deposes and subpoenas, he files the writ and
　　registers the habitual corpses.
He witnesses the jurors bailing out, the bailiff glassy-eyed, the court
　　reporter's finger stiffening from repeated movements.
He has heard family members flood the air with their tears.

He has seen the seesaw of acquittal and conviction pivoting
between yes and no.
The dead man knows that the truth may be found inside the brick
that was used as a club, on the handle of the knife that
punctured and slit, and in the handprint on the gun that
projected death, and he waits at the edge of metallurgy and
ballistics for a degree of certainty.
The dead man burns the torts and briefs mistranslated from the
past.
He stirs into the ashes of legal reasoning the unreasonable doubt of
far-fetched scenarios.
Whether the case be deliberate or accidental, he leaves nothing to
chance.
All shall be whitewashed, the stain lifted, the jury discharged
without so much as a by-your-leave from the dumbstruck.
The killer was someone else, the victims are still alive, the weapon
never existed, the alibi was too good, whatever it takes,
paranoia, conspiracy, wrongful punctuation, the jury must be
bled of its life force.
The dead man stores in time the hair, the blood, the fingerprints
and mug shots, the withdrawn shoelaces, the shackles and
cuffs, the trophies and souvenirs, the soap and tar, the
sectioned buffet tray, the precedents, the testimony and
visitations, and he wraps the severed finger in a
handkerchief to call into question whether or not this finger
was part of a hand at the time of the crime.

THE BOOK OF THE DEAD MAN (#57)

1. "HE IS NOT KAFKA AND YET HE IS KAFKA."

Like the hero of *The Trial*, the dead man is and is not.
The dead man is and is not mortal or immortal, is and is not menial
    or maximal, he has and hasn't, he says and doesn't.
By his old clothes and worn masks he seems familiar.
The dead man hid himself in view, he led the sublime down the
    garden path of public consumption, he captivated the masses
    with an empty bucket and a hoe.
Who better than the dead man to dress up like a gardener?
How can the masters and mistresses of the moment break free to
    join the roses, let the dead man do it.
The dead man serves the moment, he savors the crystalline instant,
    he relishes and reveres each subdivision of time.
Naturally, the dead man enjoys the privilege of transubstantiation
    in sight of an open door.
Inevitably and irrevocably, the dead man mates with all creatures
    familiar and unfamiliar, who crawl, fly, swim or walk, those
    who stand accused, those devoid of words, those abundant in
    rubble and salvage.
The dead man's caterer may someday serve tea in teacups too
    fragile not to be beauty itself.
The dead man's agent may someday make of light and dark, and
    nothing else, a garden beyond the grasp of prolonged sighs.

2. More About the Dead Man and Kafka

Nothing more than a white apron now holds a residue of the dead
      man's blood.

Condemned to be bathed, condemned to bleed, condemned to be
      sanctified.

The dead man offers his throat to the mirror.

He lops the curled ends from his beard, the squared ends from
      his fingernails, the bent wax from his ears and the roses
      from spring.

His is the union of the accused of another age.

His moment is dusk, his season is autumn, his time is late.

The dead man's independence counsels us to have done likewise.

His overarching abundance, worldly and other-, advises us from
      beyond.

The dead man knocks on the door as he would strike the chopping
      stone beneath his head.

He stands by the snorting carriage horses sprayed by their saliva as
      he would stand at court bathed in darkness.

The dead man is and is not an insect and a dog.

THE BOOK OF THE DEAD MAN (#58)

1. About the Dead Man Outside

They came to the door because he was small or went to some
        church or other or was seen in the company of girls or boys.
Well, he was small and went to synagogue and didn't know what to
        make of it.
They said he was from some tribe, but he didn't understand it.
They acted as if they knew what they were doing.
They were the executioners of brown eyes and brown hair, and he
        happened to have both.
Well, he said, and they went away before he awoke.
They were a dream he was having before he became the dead man.
Today the dead man lives where others died.
He passes the crematoriums without breathing.
He enters the pit graves and emerges ashen or lime-laced.
He shreds the beautiful tapestries of history and hangs in their
        place the rough shirts and dank pants forsaken at the
        showers, and the tiny work caps.
He mounts the hewn chips of shoesoles, the twisted spectacles, the
        tortured belts and suspenders, the stained handkerchiefs.
Here, he says, is history, maternity, inheritance.

2. More About the Dead Man Outside

Let none pardon the Devil lest he have to begin again.
Let no one weep easily, let no one build portfolios of disaster
        snapshots or record the lingo of the know-betters, let no one
        speak who has not considered the fatalities of geography.
The dead man does not suffer skinheads lightly, their evil is legion.
With an olive branch, he whips the villains into a frenzy of
        repentance.

The dead man tattoos the war criminals with the numbers.

The dead man wonders what America would be like if every war
were a wall engraved with the names of the lost.

Well, they said, he was from some tribe or other, and he didn't
understand it.

When the dead man was a dead child, he thought as a child.

Now the dead man lives that others may die, and dies that others
may live.

Let the victims gather, the dead man stays on the outside
looking in.

Let the saved celebrate, the dead man stands distant, remote.

The dead man listens for the sound of Fascist boots.

They will be going again to his grave to try to cut down his
family tree.

This time the dead man will see them in Hell.

THE BOOK OF THE DEAD MAN (#59)

1. About the Dead Man and Consciousness

If numb, the dead man may think himself unfeeling.
If insensate, he may think himself indifferent.
He too rides the rim trail of alternative knowledge.
He too seeks prudence and insight, and would not become an old
      bottle for new wine.
The dead man believes that he must empty himself.
Time is moving through him, unwavering, insensate.

2. More About the Dead Man and Consciousness

In the domestic alphabet, the symbol for the dead man is a
      clothespin.
Like a duck's foot, the dead man contains four wishes.
He might have been a pair of duck feet, scuffling in the
      interminable mud, but instead he became a man of
      two minds.
He might have stayed in the center of the widening gyre, but he
      became instead the new atom.
The dead man did not set out to become a crummy dummy,
      anymore than an infant sets out to become a man or woman
      of means.
The dead man is a means to an end, the later that defines the now.

THE BOOK OF THE DEAD MAN (#60)

1. About the Dead Man and Less

Now the dead man quivers with increasing abnormality.
Increasingly abnormal, the dead man is a leaking battery whose
      next spark will be the last of its life.
Those who know, know.
What was in the beam of a flashlight that the dead man shone it at
      the stars?
Whom did the dead man signal, and who replied?
The dead man reads the semaphore of comet tails and meteor
      showers.
He wanders the night sky tracing the route of Orion.
He moves a flashlight among the constellations like calipers
      measuring the expanding universe.
The dead man giveth life unto the night.
None but the dead man can so render the illusion of eternity.
Here lies the dead man, not anyotherwhere.
Nor anywhere other than here shall the dead man be seen to have
      vanished.
The dead man waves the Milky Way before him like a magician's
      handkerchief.
He grabs the moon by its ears and lowers it into his outsized
      top hat.
He enraptures the planets by repeatedly bowing, drawing them
      closer even as they lean over the precipice of their oval
      tracks.
Why did the dead man smile to think the universe egg-shaped?
The dead man tosses his flashlight from hand to hand like the
      emcee at the last night of the year.
The dead man's light is incandescent and fluorescent, it flows
      through and around him, it spots and vanquishes, it follows a
      subject from first act to last, from stage to offstage, from
      balcony to footlight.

The dead man is awash in negative space, invisible in light but
manifest on the other side of the merely dark.
He walks behind the plow as it shaves the sky of light.
The dead man does not come from this direction or that one.

2. More About the Dead Man and Less

To the dead man, all is written but not in so many words.
The dead man's voyage through space takes him to the edge of
time, the border of breath and the end of anything more.
Hence, the dead man is less than his story, a good yarn.
The dead man fesses up, he tells and implies, he hints and reveals.
The dead man's diary is replete with bite marks where he sunk his
teeth into the day.
When the dead man is thought about less, he becomes less to be
thought about.
And where the dead man took less, he takes less yet.
For the dead man is a mote and a mite, less particular than an
electron, subordinate in position to a neutron, groundless as
a light wave content to arc above earthly illumination.
What does it mean, that the dead man is less but is no less than
everything?
How can the world credit the dead man with all-or-nothing?
The dead man wagers less and less on each roll of the planet.
He wraps it up, he cashes in, but before that he so mixes up odd
and even, heads and tails, high hands and bluffs, that the
game goes under.
The dead man is a proponent of winner-take-less.

THE BOOK OF THE DEAD MAN (#61)

1. About the Dead Man and the Late Conjunctions of Fall

The dead man heard a clucking in the trees at maple-sugaring time.
Today he feels a fibrillation in the curling leaves of autumn.
The near-frost lengthens his line of sight, bringing down the moon,
     while among the spheroid melodies of harvesting, fate
     detaches the prospects.
The dead man fosters the free flying of the leaves.
He encourages deciduous trees to be done with dying.
There where the Anglo-Saxon and the Latinate meet anew, the dead
     man bespeaks the continental drift.
There where body and soul conjoin, the dead man rejoins the
     indivisible nation.
Who but the dead man can fashion a broom from a branch and
     discern the seasons from wisps of sugar and pollen?
The dead man sandpapers flakes and splinters from the chair where
     the one oblivious to time sits reading beneath burnt foliage.
He calls to the wild turkey in its infancy to stay still in the brush.
The dead man cedes supremacy neither to the body nor the soul,
     neither does he stay in one place like a day on the calendar.
The dead man feels like the tree which was tapped for syrup, all in
     good time.

2. More About the Dead Man and the Late Conjunctions of Fall

The dead man readies himself for the ice skaters whirling overhead,
     their blades crying *wish* and *wish*.
Which will crack in the brittle days to come, the dead man's ring or
     the dead man's ring finger?
The dead man does not hasten, nor does he pitch his tent.

The dead man, like others, shall be departing and returning, for such is the grandiloquence of memory in the junctures of separation.

The dead man attaches an epistle to a leaf, he discloses his whereabouts to the harvest moon, he cranks forth leaflet upon leaflet to satisfy the scene.

The dead man's dying leaves, burning, appear as a crimson wash in the autumn dusk.

His is the midnight light of high proceedings beyond the horizon.

The dead man will not twitch lest he frighten the little twigs from their exposed roosts.

When there is no holding on, no letting go, no firm grip, no restoration, no hither and yon, no arboreal refuge, then okay — say that the dead man in his vigor watches it all.

He holds his tongue lest he sound the alarm.

He hears the fallen extremities swept away by the wind and remembers.

The dead man has written an elegy for autumn and a postscript to the Apocalypse.

THE BOOK OF THE DEAD MAN (#62)

1. About the Dead Man Apart

When the dead man opens himself up, he is blown about, showered, shed, scattered, dismantled, diluted and diffused, not discarded.

When the dead man is unfolded — unbent and unbowed — he is gathered, consolidated and collected, not condensed.

The melee, the chaos, the disorder, the tumult — the dead man sleeps.

Libraries drift past laden with coffins of illusion.

Things truly dead lie buried in the commercial tide, sweep in on the sea.

The dead man is joyful in the future of his having said so.

What to do and where to be in the millennium is of the moment.

The dead man's old eyes peruse and otherwise overtake the intentions of blood on parchment, divinations and forecasts, the jubilee of a century of anticipation.

The dead man signs on and off, his silence is his assent.

His irretrievable warrant must live in the henceforth and the consequences.

His ardor shall endure, though it sag with the dew point.

The dead man too had fits of loneliness, from which he has recovered.

He sank to the depth of doubt and fell past time into vast confusion, from which he has recovered.

He slept with illusion and woke with unreality, from which he has recovered.

He made the mistake of youth, the error of age, the blunders, the bloopers, the false steps of left and right and of the deceptively wide middle way.

All the dead man wanted and wants, he has.

Where the sun has forgotten the moon, where the stars have
forsaken the abyss and the very footing has moved on, the
dead man knows his place.
The dead man is forever flagrant.

2. MORE ABOUT THE DEAD MAN APART

The dead man knows that death does not shine in the dark, as the
wind is not blown about.
It is up to the dead man to subject himself to the subjective.
It is the dead man's fate to be passionately detached.
Who, facing the end, better hikes, hurries, treks and tours?
Who but the dead man, having all the time in the world, dispatches
his intentions?
Go thou, says the dead man, thou book born in ignorance, go thou
and do likewise, otherwise, elsewise, be not timid among the
blind specialists.
The dead man does not pluck, cull or garner reality.
When there is no end result, no picaresque interval, no immediate
or impending, nothing imminent that is not also the past,
then why not roses and rubles, peace and prosperity, and
okay it's not inconsequential to have come and gone.
When the boat departed with the jackal-headed oarsman, the dead
man was here and gone.
Then the horrific was infused with beauty, and the dead man lit a
lamp.
The dead man's ashen look is the dun result of his volatile
condition.
The dead man loves you because your habits slay him, you tap your
foot to the music, and your heart blows up when you gasp.

THE BOOK OF THE DEAD MAN (#63)

1. About the Dead Man and Anyway

The dead man has up-the-stairs walking disorder.

He has one-foot-in-front-of-the-other indisposition and other
aspects of the wistful.

He has over-the-hillitis, the past-one's-prime predicament of week-
old celery or last year's universal theory.

The dead man has a pox, a condition, an affliction, the usual
entropic timing, the sudden parsimony of a reformed
spendthrift, all of it born of the purest, simplest love:
gratitude for having been.

What if the dead man's love were less, would that make your pear
wrinkle?

What if the dead man's truth were unsaid, would that cause you to
kiss yourself down there?

Come on, come off it, be upstanding, it's not all fruits and
vegetables, peaches and cream, rubber chickens or joy
buzzers.

The dead man never said he wouldn't die.

Anyway, the dead man is too alive to have been dead all this time.

The dead man is the light that was turned on to study the dark.

Where there is no more nonetheless, no before or after, no
henceforth or regardless, then the dead man in his infirmity,
deformity, and prolonged ability overlaps his beloved in
riotous whatchamacallit.

The dead man's language for love is largely blue-collar
whatchamacallit.

2. More About the Dead Man and Anyway

The dead man rubs salt in his wound anyway.
When the dead man finds in himself a hollow, he fills it with salt
      anyway.
A little torture is breathtaking for as long as the dead man can
      hold his breath.
The discomfort that will not let the dead man sit still is transformed
      into curiosity by late night abandon.
The beauty of the horrific is bled of its human cost by the long
      night of shaking.
The dead man, after long silence, sings his way through the
      graveyards.
If there is any way to change pigskin to silk, the dead man will
      find it.
Anyway, he has only one or two lives to give for his country.
He has only himself and his other self.
The dead man will not be countenanced or counterfeited, he will
      not be understood by the merely reasonable, he will not
      bleed his wounds of their hideous glamour and come up
      pristine.
Those who would slightly reorganize the bones will find their
      vanity unrewarded.
Those who would take the dead man's head away will lose
      themselves in the topography of his skull.
The dead man stands for what things are, not what you call them.
The dead man stands for living anyway.

THE BOOK OF THE DEAD MAN (#64)

1. About the Dead Man's Deathstyle

The dead man practices a healthy deathstyle.

Oh, who now can forestall the dead man's imminent passing?

What with every little thing, the dead man sits atop a system too
    gone in the gut to go on.

Now is the dead man's time to be ransacked.

Hard materialism reveals the elastic character of reincarnation:
    either the universe is finite, so nothing is ever lost, or the
    universe is infinite, so nothing is ever lost.

It appears to the dead man that not to be is still to be, yonder and
    hence.

Excuse me, whispers the dead man, elbowing past like a penitent in
    Zen vaudeville.

Forgive me, whispers the dead man, rehearsing an apology for your
    imminent long memory.

2. More About the Dead Man's Deathstyle

The dead man will last, but not for the usual reasons.

In the circumspect annals of the dead man, no dead weight, no
    interlude that does not assert its count, no residue that does
    not rise to embody, no line on the oscilloscope that does not
    jump for joy.

The dead man has been *there*, and he's been *here*, and he likes it
    here.

Thawed blood flows back into numbed limbs.

A jumpy pulse increasingly interrupts the horizontal.

The brain's whirligig, each organ collects or refuses according to its
    purpose, each sensory aperture widens to receive the stimuli
    put on hold.

The dead man is shapely to surrender, trim to relinquish, tidy for
the final presentation.
Let the grass flagellate the earth, still the dead man lingers.
Let the wind tug the hair shirt of the burial site, the dead man
tarries.
Let the sky bend to see what gives, still the dead man does not give
ground all at once.
The dead man cannot be done with, for his register and chronicle,
his yarns and recitals, his rosters of lives shall be obsessively
and incautiously annotated.
It is the dead man's way, for his penchant and proclivity have made
of the green reed a whistle on which to solo.

THE BOOK OF THE DEAD MAN (#65)

1. About the Dead Man and Sense

The dead man struggles not to become crabby, chronic or
    hypothetical.
He searches philosophy in vain for a pair of boots, a butterfly, a
    bent nail, an overlooked umbrella, some paste or scalp oil,
    but these new professors are all talk.
To the dead man, their theories are a kind of fretting, a way of
    blaming, a rightness carried to wrongheadedness, they have
    each other.
The dead man steps repeatedly into the stream, he does not wait for
    the water to be recycled.
His inclination is all downhill.
That's why the dead man likes all weather.
At bank's edge, he sees punk weed, tadpoles, pebbles that speak
    with mouths full of water, mud fit to be balm.
The water is less than it was to a fetus, but more than it will be.
How can the dead man explain water to these oversubscribed, arid
    phlegmatics?
A little water in the palm is worth the windpipes of a thousand
    tutors.
Helen Keller among these by-the-book tutors might still be waiting
    for a word.
Whitman's learned astronomer still prattles on about the distant
    stars, which for the dead man are at arm's reach.
The dead man laughs to see cold water thrown on language by
    those who are nourished by praise.
Their too many words have made a soupy alphabet.

2. MORE ABOUT THE DEAD MAN AND SENSE

It would be wrong of the dead man to blame earth, water, fire or
    air.
It would be foolish to hold others hostage for a ransom that never
    existed.
It would be inescapably topsy-turvy to hold up to censure the
    material or the immaterial, the psychical or spiritual, the
    mental or emotional.
How curious now are the dead man's postures, struck in the dark
    for worms.
What on earth did the dead man imagine his frothiest words to be
    worth?
When there is no safe passage, no carriage wings, no golden ladder,
    no river to cross, no sage, no idiot, no ratchet-wheel big
    enough or lever long enough then okay the dead man no
    longer strives to move the earth.
He would be one with missteps and failures, of a piece with error
    and fault, united with blemish and blunder.
He would be, and he is.
The dead man's thought is visceral and unconditional, love as it was
    intended when the river met the shore.

THE BOOK OF THE DEAD MAN (#66)

1. About the Dead Man and Everpresence

That one was lost at sea and another to rot, that one threw himself
    from a roof and another from a bridge, and that he, of these
    and others, deferred and delayed has been a long
    astonishment to the dead man.
That he should be the green soul is a shock and a stupefaction.
To what end was it begotten that he be known among his late
    friends?
Why hath he not perished as studiously as prophecy foretold?
He has pals, but not so many now, who, borderlines, go their own
    ways.
When there is no more sacred or heretical, no promise, no
    guarantee, no warrant that places the millennium, no voltage
    too high or current too strong, then naturally there can be
    no one side, no one alone, no other and no otherwise.
Loam or grime, clay or dust, the dead man penetrates and
    permeates, he pervades and saturates and otherwise occupies
    every veneer, wrapper and façade.
Likewise, he hath gone dry in the leaves to better touch them.

2. More About the Dead Man and Everpresence

Shall the dead man doubt the ax or the envelope, the tar or the
    hinge, the birthday candle or the rubbery moon?
It is longer and longer that things are as they are.
Shall he ask the river to be a capsule, the shoesole to be a clockface,
    the library paste to be rivets?
The dead man knows that the owl's hoot is also a searchlight, that
    an enamel doorhandle may become a beacon, that milk is
    also bone meal.

66

To be at all, the Whitmaniacal wonder of it, the Homeric – harsh
　　register this age has come to, with all its data.
To be unknowing, through martial times or Chaucerian –
　　soul-searing these days have been upon us.
The dead man leaves among the burned shirts, the shredded
　　insulation, the free gases and syrups, amidst the upturned
　　and rooted-out, hints of a trail made of basic materials.
Do not let them tell you that the dead man has gone on ahead.

THE BOOK OF THE DEAD MAN (#67)

1. About the Dead Man's Further Happiness

If truth begins in heresy, then the dead man's capacity is the root
cause.

If the future is famished, if every angel is terrible, then the dead man's
appetite is to blame.

Tuber or bulb, grit or grub – the dead man is not above a bit the
amalgamate malarkey of the underworld.

To the dead man, the abyss is not the pit it was said to be, but is
elsewise and otherwise.

The dead man's refusal to mourn is notorious, gladly has he traveled
in stateless realms: child of a universal Diaspora.

The dead man's shoes are too muddy, too shabby, to have been left to
chance.

Do not assume, what with his high jinks and horseplay, that the dead
man has not sometimes had the smile wiped from his face
(Mister).

He, too, has been made to wish he was someone or somewhere else.

He, too, has been told to suffer in silence.

Yet he has flourished under the gun, been free in his chains, ducked
and sidestepped his captors without moving.

To the dead man in solitary, alone with his thoughts, the world was
two things at once.

Why is he, root cause and effect, happy and was he?

And why was he happy – and is he?

The dead man confounds the carriers of salt water who hang about
looking for open wounds.

He misleads the bullies, the roughriders, the toughs and the thugs, he
defuses, he disengages, he acquits, discharges and absolves.

The dead man's behavior befits the nearly departed, the temporarily
indisposed, the tailored by-product of our declination – here
and gone in a jiffy, in a twinkling, in a flash.

Ah bliss, that fairly glories in the grave and the ephemeral.
Ah sensible gladness, that reflects equally the divisible and the
divine.
For it is the dead man who recalls the sea to the shoreline where
sandpipers print the beach.
And it is the dead man who summons from the ocean floor the clay
to make the stone egg that safeguards the fossil.
For the dead man's rogue ruminations get under his skin, he
worries and pleases himself equally – parent and child.
Yet his unhappiness was turned round as if it had met a wall and
could go no further.
The dead man in his earthly joy has taken transcendence down
a peg.

2. More About the Dead Man's Further Happiness

That he wanted to be there and not there was to him to feel desire
doubly.
That he wished twice as hard was to him to manifest a method
to his madness.
The dead man must be doubly peaceful to know peace.
He must be twice as ecstatic to fathom himself orgasmic.
He must be two times the man he was, twin to a twin, a voice
congruent with its echo – twice cursed, twice blessed.
The dead man sees the armored crab take to the bait.
He smiles to see the bait take the crab and the tide turn tail.
He hears the slatted sides of his craft complaining to the waves.
He laughs to hear the salt water wearing away its knuckles.

The dead man risks the peril of your affection for a laugh that is
   also a yawp and a howl, and the hail that is also farewell.
Where there is no second sight, no reconsideration, no
   disconnection of wishes granted from dreams deferred, then
   okay good sense is sensory and grief a wispy exhalation of
   melancholia.
He who became the dead man was made to feel doubly: active and
   detached, refreshed and depleted.
The dead man's ups-and-downs are to him private peaks and valleys
   measured by their distance from the moon.

THE BOOK OF THE DEAD MAN (#68)

1. Accounts of the Dead Man

The dead man likes it when the soup simmers and the kettle hisses.
He wants to live as much as possible at the ends of his fingertips.
To make sense, to make nonsense, to make total sense, lasting sense,
　　ephemeral sense, giddy sense, perfect sense, holy sense.
The dead man wants it, he requires it, he trusts it.
Therefore, the dead man takes up with words as if they had
　　nowhere in mind.
The dead man's words are peacock feathers, bandages, all the
　　everyday exotica ground under by utility.
The dead man's book foresees a flickering awareness, an ember
　　at the end of the Void, a glitter, a glow beneath the ash.
The dead man's book is the radical document of time, nodding
　　to calamity and distress, happy in harm's way.
To the dead man, the mere whistling of a pedestrian may signal
　　an onslaught of intention.
The dead man calls his spillover a journal because it sounds
　　helpless and private, while a diary suggests the writings
　　of someone awaiting rescue.
The dead man doesn't keep a diary.
The dead man sweeps under the bed for scraps, pieces, chips, tips,
　　fringework, lace, filings and the rivets that rattled and broke.
His is a flurry of nothing-more-to-give, the echo of a prolonged
　　note struck at the edge of an inverted bowl.
Now he must scrub his brain before a jury of his peers.

2. More Accounts of the Dead Man

The dead man has caused a consternation, but he didn't mean to.
He was just clocking his pulse, tracking his heart, feeling his way.
He was just dispersing the anomalous and otherwise scouting the
     self-evident and inalienable.
It was just that sometimes he couldn't stand it because he was
     happy.
It was the effect that he effected that affected him.
Some say it was his fervor for goose bumps took his breath away.
Some say it was the dead man's antsiness that put him in the dirt.
Some say he was too much the live wire, the living will, the holy
     spirit, the damn fool.
His was a great inhalation, wanton, a sudden swivel in the midst of
     struggle, a death dance with demons and other dagnabbits.
The dead man was well into physical geezerhood when he came to a
     conclusion and declared his independence.
At once he was chockablock with memories, the progeny of design
     and of blooper, boner and glitch.
He had his whole life to live.
When there is no more beseeching or gratitude, no seats remaining
     on the metaphysical seesaw, no zero-sum activity, no
     acquisition that is not also a loss, no finitude, then of course
     the dead man smiles as he blows a kiss through the wispy
     curtain of closure.
Some say the dead man was miserable to be so happy.

THE BOOK OF THE DEAD MAN (#69)

1. In Which the Dead Man Speaks for Himself

Conclusively, concussively, decidedly – the dead man went beyond
    to reach the limitless.
Love, faith, that which does good or harm, that which is neutral,
    that which is dispensable, the selfhood of the artist, the
    selfless sage – the dead man admits to being but one of
    many.
That there is still ego in observation, that there is yet self in the
    mildest awareness of another – he cannot go further except
    he go no further.
I shall be speaking of the dead man with shut eyes and a writhing
    brain besides.
I shall have to lay my head on a pillow.
It was the Army way through the long trench until he held, facing
    the guns under bullet-tracings in a night sky.
One of many.
The dead man went over the top and beyond the pale.
He evened things up, he squared the odds, he made sense of
    rubbish and folly.
He was rapt and aroused, he was himself, within and without.
He was my particular and my universal.
I leave it to the future to say why.

2. In Which the Dead Man Speaks Again for Himself

That there was an I who saw it all –
When they poisoned the well, I babbled at the brook.
That one lived at the expense of another.
Always the last hoard of food, the final barrel of sterile water, and
    one solution was as good as the next.

The dead man notes the brilliant holding action, the rigor, that is
civilization.

The dead man sponges up its literature and art, he travels in Space
and observes microcosmic innards without his presence
distorting the works within.

But the dead man cannot do this to himself forever.

The cows are out there but they won't come home.

Hell's fires are banked but they will not freeze.

Was he not, forage and the Devil besides, the happiest dead man
alive?

I thank him, whom I shall not see again in this life.

He makes me smile.

THE BOOK OF THE DEAD MAN (#70)

1. ABOUT THE DEAD MAN AND THE PICKET FENCE

Ten to one, the one in question made it home safely.
Everyone was glad the party was over, and the séance had ceased
      that was seeking the lost art of conversation.
The three metaphysicians left early.
The seven alchemists did not come out of the kitchen all evening.
No one brought up the red leaves of sunset, there was not a
      hangnail to be seen, nor were shoes mentioned, nor saw
      blades nor carburetors, nor a pencil with an eraser nor the
      shell of a crab nor the imaginary eyebrow of a
      hummingbird.
It was as if a world without turtles hastened time, and it took a
      universe free of glue, spittle and the secretions of bees to
      tour space.
A world without means or ends, a world of process without a
      project.

2. MORE ABOUT THE DEAD MAN AND THE PICKET FENCE

Always to be the swirl blown into the bottom of the glass bowl, the
      finger marks on the stoneware, the ember that went upward
      as the kiln fire reached cone ten.
The dead man reconstitutes the story of the blind man who could
      see, the deaf man who could hear, the mute who could speak.
Nor scuttlebutt, nor buzz, nor yarn – reports of a dead man who
      lives have been documented.
The dead man was seen scraping gum from the sole of his shoe.
His wool cap and thick trousers were glimpsed going down an alley.
He was seen from a distance placing a white egg on a picket fence
      where no one would see it.
His presence was detected in a darkened movie house.

He was observed without his knowing making snowmen and mud
      pies, sand castles and leaf piles.
His fingerprints appeared in the clay.
He was seen trying not to be seen the day the sky fell.
Everyone loves the shine of the ordinary, the dead man too.
All may study the rainbow, the dead man also.
Not a man or woman does not envy the owl its privacy, the dead
      man besides.

ABOUT THE POET

Marvin Bell was born in New York City and grew up in Center Moriches, on the south shore of eastern Long Island. Since 1985 he has divided his time between Iowa City, Iowa, and Port Townsend, Washington. He is the author of thirteen distinguished books of poetry and essays.

BOOK DESIGN & composition by John D. Berry Design, using Adobe PageMaker 6.0, a
Power 120, and a Macintosh IIVX. The text typeface is Berthold Bodoni Antiqua
Medium, and the display type on the title page and the cover is FF Bodoni Classic. The
wide variety of typefaces created by Giambattista Bodoni in the late 18th century set
the standard for the "modern" style of type, with its extreme variation between thick
and thin strokes and the strictly vertical orientation of its letters. The most influential
of the 20th-century revivals was ATF Bodoni, designed for the American Type
Founders by Morris F. Benton and issued in 1910–1911. Benton's version differed in
many details from Bodoni's originals, especially in its stark, unbracketed serifs, but
the clean regularity of the ATF face appealed to the spirit of modern printing in the
early 20th century, and most of the currently available Bodoni revivals are based on
Benton's design. H. Berthold AG issued its version in 1930, based on a Haas copy of
the Benton type, then adapted it for photocomposition in the 1970s, under the
direction of Günter Gerhard Lange. Despite this long history of adaptation, Berthold's
Bodoni Antiqua is respected as one of the most useful of the "mechanical" revivals of
Bodoni. ¶ FF Bodoni Classic, by contrast, is based directly on examples of Giam-
battista Bodoni's types, and it retains many of the unusual details of the originals,
such as delicately bracketed serifs and the unique ball-serif on the tail of the
capital R. Bodoni Classic was designed by Gert Wiescher and
issued by FontShop International in 1993.
Printed by McNaughton & Gunn.